FIRE IN THE BUSHVELD

Grandma Goes to

South Africa series

Linda L. Sheehan

DEDICATION

To my brave son Daniel, who time and again led the volunteers (including his dad) on our farm into
the South African blazes and helped to save farms, homes, and animals.
You are an amazing son!

ACKNOWLEDGMENTS

Thanks to Matthew Rhine for pictures of the South African fires that he also fought alongside Daniel and Dennis. Special thanks to Gondwana Tours and Safaris of Botswana for some great photos.
Visit them at http://www.gondwanatoursandsafaris.com.
Special thanks to Angela Onuma and Celia Milslagle for proofreading and recommendations, and my niece Katie Onuma for helping with the pictures and book cover.   I greatly appreciate all of you.

BEST FRIENDS FOREVER

    Woodlands cover most of the Limpopo Province of the South African bushveld. Trees and bushes dot the grassy plains.

    This is home to Momma, Papa, and Baby James, the zebra family. They live on a large game reserve. A herd of elands often graze with the zebras. Winter time is very dry. They find little to eat.

Spring brings rain. The temperature grows warmer. The thick, green grass pops up. Baby James and his mother calmly graze in the bushveld. The elands, elephants, and many other animals join them.

Baby James likes to trot happily beside his mother. He sees new things every day. He is always curious. His own shadow surprises him!

Yesterday Baby James saw a strange, tall animal. Its long neck reached to the top of the tree. Baby James looked up, up, up. The mother giraffe munched the leaves. Baby James watched her carefully.

What a long throat! Finally, he followed her neck down, down, down to her legs. There, asleep at her feet, was Baby Justine.

Suddenly, Baby Justine jumped up. She had a big smile and very different fur. She was tiny compared to her mother. In fact, she could even walk underneath her mother! For a moment, Baby James was scared. He leaped back. "Hhh hi," he finally whispered.

Baby Justine steadied herself on her long legs. She stared at Baby James. She had never seen a zebra before. Her mother's voice reminded her that everything was just fine.

"You have spots and I have stripes," said Baby James bravely. "Can we be friends?"

Baby James and Baby Justine grew to be best friends forever. New discoveries and adventures met them every day in the bushveld.

The spring sunlight warmed them at sunrise. They ran with the morning breeze as it danced across the bushveld. In the evening they splashed in the nearby river.

Hunger often interrupted their play. But that was no problem. Their mothers always stayed nearby. The lively little babies both grew up quickly.

Summer will soon arrive. In just a little while, the weather will be very hot. The bushveld will turn into an uncomfortable and even dangerous place for all. The lovely sunshine will change to burning heat. It will blaze down on everyone.

The waterbuck family huddles together during the cold nights. They are always in large groups.

The water buffalo and warthogs also adjust to the changing weather. Now the days are pleasant and the nights near freezing. It is spring and change is in the air.

FIRE IN THE BUSHVELD

The farmers' fields are also in the bushveld. Farmers are always busy planting, reaping, or caring for their crops. Sometimes the animals can see the men working. Baby James and Baby Justine soon learn not to wander near the fence. They only watch the men from far away.

One sunny morning Baby Justine looked up. The beautiful mountains that surrounded the animals did not look the same. Why were they different today? She went to ask her father.

"Yes, Justine," her father asked, "what's the problem?"

"I know about raindrops," said Baby Justine. "I know what rain clouds look like too. But look over there, Papa. What is that dark cloud doing in the trees?"

Baby Justine's father raised his head. Smoke! Fire! Danger!

Just at that moment a loud clap of thunder sounded. Baby Justine jumped in fear and stood trembling. Lightning flashed nearby and she screeched in surprise.

"Justine, go to your mother," said her father.

"Yes, Papa!" Baby Justine obeyed without question.

The fire was small right now. The thick, dreadful smoke rose like a fat serpent in the air. These flames could soon threaten their home here in the bushveld. Father must warn the other animals.

The fire spread quickly. Now they could see the smoke behind the farmer's house. What will the farmer do? Can he put out the fire? Can he help the animals?

The fierce winds whipped the sparks into the air. They flew across the road. New fires were starting everywhere. At times the flames looked like tornadoes. The fire ate up everything in its path.

In just a few hours the inferno had spread across the bushveld. The animals were in great danger. Will the fire come to their game reserve? Can they escape the flames?

Soon the animals heard the tractor's roaring engine. The farmer is plowing up part of his field. He is making a fire break. Freshly turned soil will not burn. Now the flames will not spread further into the bushveld.

Other farmers jumped in their water trucks. They were prepared for the dangerous lightning fires. They took their water sprayers. These brave men went to put out these fires that so often come in the spring.

Baby James, Baby Justine, and the other families stared at the smoke. They could see it and smell it. The flames continued to inch closer and closer. The animals waited nervously and watched.

The fire crept nearer to the giraffes, zebras, and other animals. They all raced to the far corner of the game reserve. Baby James and Baby Justine huddled with their parents. They could not jump over the fence.

One elephant family played in the mud. Suddenly, Mother elephant smelled smoke! Everyone got up quickly. They all ran for their lives.

Many animals ran madly here and there. It was a frenzy. They feared the flames and the smoke. Tiny animals got away through the fences. The larger animals could not escape. The game reserve fence held them captive.

Suddenly the lion cubs woke up. They did not like what they saw and smelled. They ran with their mother to the corner of the game reserve. Still, the fence stopped them from getting away.

Flames traveled quickly up and down the mountains. The firefighters needed extra help.

Some noisy helicopters came to pour chemicals on the fires. Other helicopters and aircraft dumped water on the flames. They worked together with the farmers. All the same, the fire kept spreading.

Even with all the help, the fire destroyed a lot. Some people lost their homes and buildings. Big and small animals lost their homes too. The crusty, dry bushveld had quickly turned black. The grassy fields were now scarred and smoky.

The farmers did not forget about Baby James, Baby Justine and their animal friends. Before long some firefighters came to cut open the fence in the corner of the game reserve. They quickly let the animals run to a safer place.

Now they were out of harm's way. Soon they all calmed down and silently watched the bushveld burn.

BURNING THROUGH THE NIGHT

The flames grew brighter as the sun went down. Total darkness finally came. The fire was not put out yet. It would be a long night for the courageous men and women.

This firefighter surveys the fire line approaching the farm.

People from all over came to help. Some firefighters did not have water to spray on the fire. They used branches and whatever they could find to beat out the flames.

The men and women fought the flames through the night. They did not go home to eat. They were tired but they did not sleep. In spite of everything, they did not stop. They would protect the bushveld the best they could.

Firefighters had a strategy to stop the fire. Hurriedly, they set backfires where possible. These new fires helped to control the burning. Flames could travel no further when they met the ground already burned by backfires. Still, the fire spread for miles and miles.

The animals could see the flames on their mountain from their new place of safety. The fire now covered a huge area.

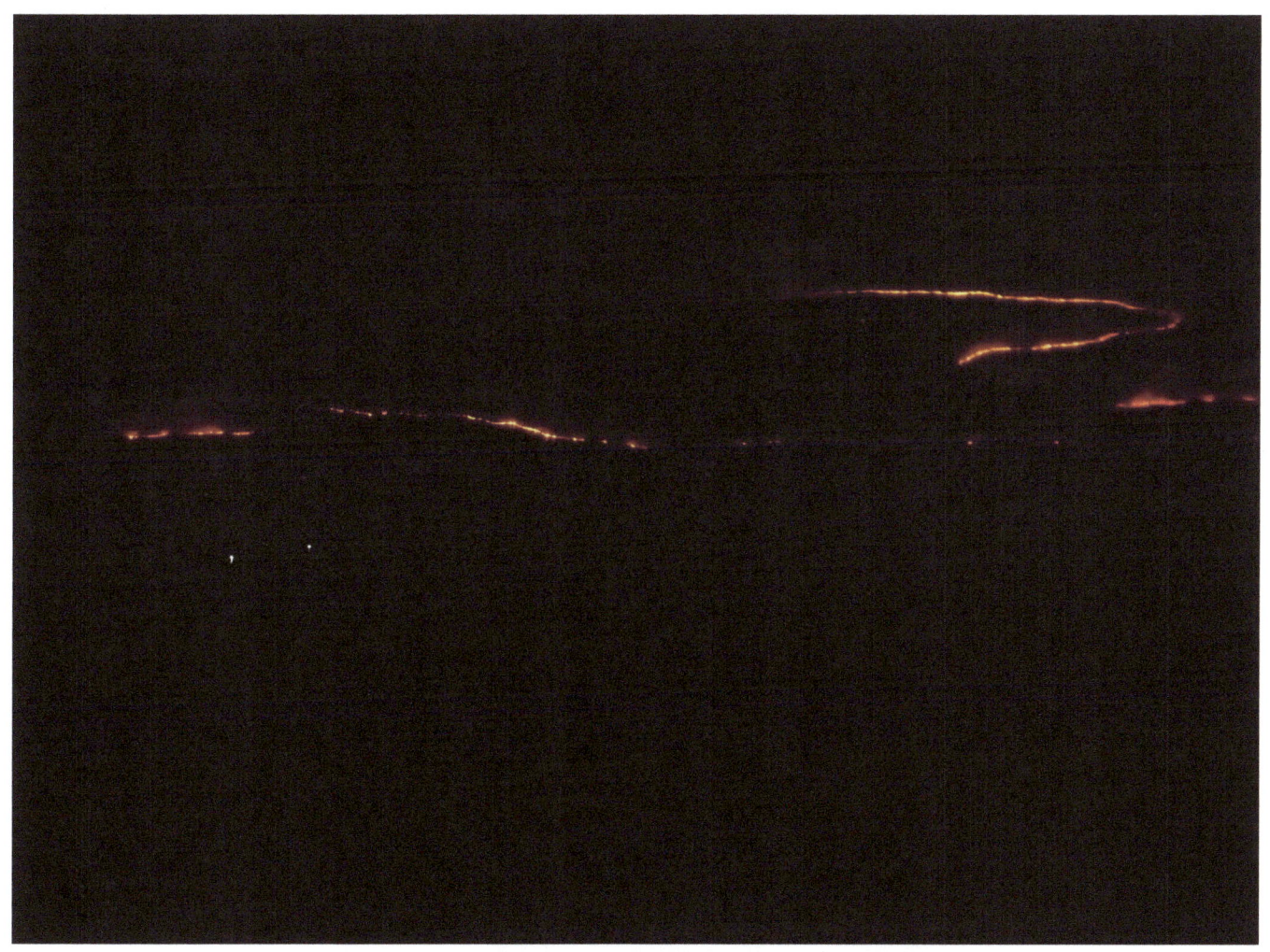

It was very dark in the bushveld after the sun went down. The fire in the mountains looked like a red serpent. It burned all night. Around 5 a.m. the weary firefighters could finally go home. They are real heroes.

A weary firefighter

AFTER THE FIRE

The next morning everyone could see the damage. Stinky smoke still swirled out of the ashes.

Baby James, Baby Justine, and their animal friends will not return to their game reserve for a while. The fires had burned the old, dry grass. Dead trees had also disappeared.

Springtime in South Africa brings rain. It also brings lightning. The bolts of lightning often start bushveld fires. It can be a dangerous time for animals and people.

After time and more rain, the bushveld will turn green again. The grass will grow tall. New bushes and grass will soon sprout in the bushveld. Summer will also come. Baby James, Baby Justine, and their animal friends can go home again.

The farmers can return to their farming. They will plant their seeds. They will irrigate their crops. All the time they will be on the lookout for smoke in the mountains.

South African farmers are ready to fight fires at all times. They are alert and watching for them every year. Their trucks and equipment are always standing by. Preparing in advance helps them put out fires more quickly.

They never forget about helping the animals in a fire. They stop fires from destroying animal homes too. Many animals survive because firefighters rescue them. Sadly, many also die.

The animals will soon dine on thick, green grass again. The trees will blossom. Snakes, rats and other small animals will return to the game reserve.

Baby James will continue to grow and trot happily beside his mother. Adventure is certainly a part of his life in South Africa.

Baby Justine will keep growing and growing and growing. She will also face many new adventures and challenges in her life in the bushveld.